THE WILD JOURNEY: EXPLORING THE HIDDEN CORNERS OF EARTH

First edition. December 23, 2024.

ISBN: 979-8227541130

Written by Anila Asif.

The Wild Journey: Exploring the Hidden Corners of Earth

Chapter 1:
Into the Heart of the Amazon Rainforest

Maya and Liam had always dreamed of going on a big adventure, but nothing could have prepared them for the journey that awaited them deep in the Amazon Rainforest. Their guide, Ana, a local biologist who knew the forest like the back of her hand, led them through the thick jungle.

The air was heavy with humidity, and the sounds of the forest were a constant buzz of life—bird calls, the rustling of leaves, and the occasional distant roar of a jaguar.

As they ventured deeper into the rainforest, Maya and Liam marveled at the incredible diversity of species around them. Brightly colored macaws soared high above, their vivid blue and red feathers creating a burst of color against the green backdrop of trees.

The rainforest was alive with the sound of wildlife, from the constant chirps of insects to the gentle movements of sloths hanging lazily from the trees. They even spotted a family of capybaras, the world's largest rodents, wading through a quiet stream.

Ana explained that the Amazon is one of the most biodiverse places on Earth. Over 400 billion trees grow here, and the rainforest is home to more than 10% of the world's known species.

This diversity is what keeps the ecosystem balanced, and many of the plants and animals play critical roles in regulating the planet’s climate. Maya and Liam learned that the Amazon is often called "the lungs of the Earth" because it absorbs large amounts of carbon dioxide and produces oxygen, helping to mitigate climate change.

But despite its importance, the rainforest is in danger.

As they continued their trek, Ana shared the harsh truth about deforestation. Every year, large sections of the Amazon are cut down for agriculture, logging, and mining. Entire habitats are being destroyed, threatening not only the creatures living there but also the delicate balance of the forest itself. The deforestation contributes to climate change, as the trees that once absorbed carbon are now gone, releasing more carbon into the atmosphere.

Maya and Liam felt a deep sense of urgency as they learned about the damage being done to this vital ecosystem. They asked Ana what they could do to help. Ana smiled, reminding them that even small actions—like supporting sustainable products and raising awareness about deforestation—could make a big difference. She also pointed out that preserving places like the Amazon is not only important for the environment but also for the people who depend on the forest for their livelihoods.

As the sun began to set, casting an orange glow across the canopy, Maya and Liam sat by the campfire, reflecting on all they had learned. The jungle around them seemed even more alive as the night creatures began to stir. They knew their adventure had just begun, and the more they learned about the Amazon, the more determined they became to protect it. They realized that the heart of the Amazon wasn't just in the trees

and animals—it was in the people who were working every day to safeguard this extraordinary place for future generations.

In the distance, the calls of howler monkeys echoed through the trees, and the friends knew that the rainforest had many more secrets waiting to be uncovered.

Chapter 2:
Climbing the Peaks of the Himalayas

After their adventure in the Amazon, Maya and Liam's next destination was the towering peaks of the Himalayas, a place that seemed as distant and mystical as the snow-capped mountains themselves. They arrived in Nepal, the gateway to the Himalayas, where the air was crisp and cool compared to the humid rainforest they had just left behind. Their guide,

Raj, a seasoned mountaineer from the local Sherpa community, greeted them warmly and prepared them for their trek into the world's highest mountain range. As they started their journey, the terrain quickly became rugged. Steep cliffs, narrow paths, and dense forests of rhododendron and pine surrounded them. Maya and Liam marveled at the breathtaking views of the snow-capped peaks, especially Mount Everest,

which towered above them like a silent giant. The air was thinner here, and they had to adjust to the altitude, taking it slow and steady to avoid altitude sickness. Raj explained that in these high-altitude ecosystems, life is harsh, and both plants and animals must adapt to survive.

Along the way, they encountered yaks—large, shaggy animals that were used by locals to carry supplies through the rugged terrain. The yaks' thick fur helped them survive in the freezing temperatures, and their sturdy hooves allowed them to navigate the rocky paths. Maya was fascinated by their strength and resilience, especially as they passed by a herd grazing on the sparse vegetation near a mountain stream.

As they climbed higher, Raj pointed out tracks in the snow that belonged to snow leopards—one of the most elusive and endangered animals in the region. Liam was excited by the possibility of spotting one of these magnificent creatures, but Raj explained that snow leopards are masters of camouflage and tend to avoid human contact. Still, the idea that such a powerful predator roamed the mountains added a sense of mystery to their journey. However, as they trekked deeper into the mountains, they learned that the region's beauty was under threat. Raj shared that the glaciers of the Himalayas, which had been slowly growing for centuries,

were now rapidly melting due to climate change. The once-solid glaciers, which feed into the rivers that supply water to millions of people, were retreating at an alarming rate. This had serious consequences for the local communities, many of which rely on glacial meltwater for drinking, farming, and hydropower.

Maya and Liam saw the effects of this firsthand. Along the path, they passed dry riverbeds that should have been flowing with fresh water from the glaciers.

In some places, the rivers had become unpredictable, flooding villages one year and running dry the next. Local farmers had to adapt by changing their crop patterns, while some villages were working together to build water storage systems to prepare for the erratic flow.

Raj also told them about the local efforts to conserve the environment. The government and several NGOs had launched programs to educate communities about sustainable farming practices and the importance of protecting the region's fragile ecosystem.

Some villages had started planting trees to reduce soil erosion and preserve the water supply, while others were working with scientists to monitor the glaciers and track changes over time. Maya felt a sense of urgency as she realized how interconnected everything was. The people, the animals, the plants, and even the glaciers were all part of a delicate balance that was now being disrupted. She and Liam discussed how the melting glaciers weren't just a local issue—they were a global one. If the glaciers continued to shrink, the effects would be felt worldwide, particularly in areas downstream that relied on the water they provided. As they reached a high vantage point on the trek, Maya and Liam stood in awe of the vast mountain range before them. The peaks seemed to touch the sky, and the beauty of the landscape left them speechless.

But they also knew that the Himalayas, like so many other natural wonders around the world, needed protection. The threats from climate change were real, and the more they learned about the challenges facing the region, the more committed they became to helping spread the message of conservation. That night, as they camped beneath the stars, the cold mountain air filled their lungs.

The distant sound of avalanches echoed from the peaks, a reminder that the mountains were constantly changing. Maya and Liam knew that their adventure wasn't just about witnessing the wonders of the Himalayas, but about understanding the challenges these ecosystems faced and the role they could play in protecting them.

As the campfire flickered out, Raj told them stories of Sherpa ancestors who had navigated these same peaks for generations, always in harmony with the land. Maya and Liam felt a deep respect for the people and wildlife of the Himalayas, and a renewed sense of responsibility to protect the planet's most precious natural treasures.

Chapter 3:
The Secret Life of the Ocean

After their high-altitude adventures in the Himalayas, Maya and Liam were ready for a new type of exploration —under the sea. Their next stop was the Great Barrier Reef off the coast of Australia, one of the most stunning and diverse ecosystems on Earth. Upon arriving, they were introduced to Emma, a marine biologist who had been studying the reef for years.

Emma explained that the Great Barrier Reef is home to over 1,500 species of fish, 400 types of coral, and countless other creatures, making it one of the most vibrant and diverse marine environments in the world. Maya and Liam were immediately captivated by the idea of diving into the crystal-clear waters to discover what lay beneath the surface. After a brief safety lesson and getting their diving gear ready, they were ready to go. As they descended into the water, the world around them transformed. The sun's rays filtered through the water, casting shimmering beams of light onto the colorful coral below. Fish darted through the reef in every color of the rainbow, and Liam was particularly excited to see a school of bright yellow butterfly fish swimming together in perfect harmony.

Emma guided them through the reef, explaining the importance of the coral and the marine life that relied on it. Coral reefs are sometimes called the "rainforests of the sea" because of their rich biodiversity, and they act as a crucial habitat for many species. They protect coastlines from storms, support fisheries, and are a source of food and shelter for countless marine species. Maya was amazed by the complexity of the reef, where each species had a specific role—some species of fish cleaned parasites off other animals, while others, like the parrotfish, helped keep algae in check by grazing on it.

But as they swam deeper into the reef, Emma's tone shifted as she explained the growing threats to this fragile ecosystem. Coral bleaching was one of the biggest dangers the reef faced. Maya and Liam learned that when sea temperatures rise due to climate change,

the corals become stressed and expel the colorful algae that live within them. This algae is vital to the corals, as it provides them with food through photosynthesis. Without the algae, the coral turns white and becomes vulnerable to disease and death. In many areas of the Great Barrier Reef, large swaths of coral had already bleached, and some parts of the reef were showing signs of irreversible damage.

"Coral reefs are incredibly sensitive to changes in the environment," Emma explained, "and warming ocean temperatures, pollution, and overfishing all play a part in their decline." As they continued exploring, Liam was shocked to see some areas of the reef that had been damaged by human activity. In some parts, they found discarded fishing nets and plastic debris, reminders of how pollution was affecting the underwater world.

The duo was disturbed but determined to learn more about what they could do to help.

The next part of their adventure involved assisting Emma and her team with a project to help protect sea turtles, which also depended on the reef. Emma led them to a small sandy beach where a group of researchers was waiting to tag newly hatched sea turtles. These turtles had emerged from their nests on the beach just hours earlier, and the team was ready to track them to study their movements in the wild. Maya and Liam were excited to help.

They carefully picked up the tiny turtles and attached small, harmless tracking devices to their shells. As the turtles were released into the ocean, Maya and Liam felt a deep sense of wonder watching the baby sea turtles make their way into the water, where they would face many dangers,

from predators to pollution. Emma explained that by tracking the turtles, scientists could gather important data about their migration patterns, which would help in protecting their habitats. The experience of helping with the turtle tagging was eye-opening for Maya and Liam. They realized that every creature, from the tiniest fish to the majestic sea turtle, played an essential role in maintaining the health of the ocean.

Without healthy coral reefs, the marine life that depended on them would struggle to survive.

Emma also shared some good news—there were ongoing efforts to protect the Great Barrier Reef. Local communities, scientists, and governments were working together to reduce overfishing, create marine protected areas, and raise awareness about the importance of coral conservation.

Maya and Liam learned about the critical work being done to reduce carbon emissions and combat climate change, which was one of the main drivers of ocean warming and coral bleaching.

As they returned to the shore, Maya and Liam felt both inspired and empowered. They understood that while the challenges facing the ocean were immense, there were still ways to make a positive impact. They pledged to continue learning about ocean conservation and to do their part to help protect the seas.

That night, as they sat on the beach and watched the stars twinkle above, Maya reflected on the adventure. The ocean was vast and mysterious, and they had only scratched the surface of understanding its true beauty and importance. But they knew that the more people learned about the challenges the oceans faced, the more hope there was for the future. And with that thought, they fell asleep under the soft glow of the moon, knowing they had contributed to the protection of one of the planet's most precious ecosystems.

Chapter 4:
In the Deserts of Africa

Maya and Liam's next adventure took them to one of the most extreme and awe-inspiring landscapes on Earth —the Sahara Desert, the largest hot desert in the world. They arrived in northern Africa, where the vast stretches of golden sand seemed to go on forever. The sun beat down relentlessly, making the air shimmer and the horizon look like it was melting into the sky.

Their guide, Khalid, a local scientist with years of experience studying desert ecosystems, welcomed them and began to explain how life in such a harsh environment managed to survive.

As Maya and Liam set out into the desert, they were immediately struck by its vastness. The sand dunes, some of which could reach up to 500 feet high, seemed like mountains of sand. But beneath the desert's seemingly barren surface, Khalid explained that the Sahara was far from lifeless.

Despite its extreme temperatures, which could soar above 120°F (49°C) during the day and plummet below freezing at night, the desert was full of remarkable creatures and plants that had adapted to survive these harsh conditions.

They soon encountered a group of camels, known as the "ships of the desert." These animals were perfectly designed for the desert life.

Khalid explained that camels could go for days without water, thanks to their unique physiology. Their thick fur protected them from the sun, while their wide, padded feet helped them navigate the soft, shifting sands without sinking. Maya and Liam were fascinated by the camels' ability to survive in such a tough environment. They learned that camels are crucial for transportation and trade in the desert, and many local people rely on them for their livelihoods. As they continued their trek, they spotted a few desert snakes slithering across the sand. Khalid pointed out a sidewinder rattlesnake, which had evolved special methods for moving across the hot sand, leaving only a series of twisting tracks behind it. He explained how many desert animals, like reptiles, had adapted to conserve moisture and regulate their body temperature.

Maya and Liam marveled at how every animal and plant in the desert seemed to have a special trick for surviving. One of the most surprising things Maya and Liam discovered was the desert's flora. Though the Sahara might appear empty and barren at first glance, it was home to several types of plants that had developed unique survival strategies. Khalid showed them a small patch of hardy shrubs with thick, waxy leaves designed to trap moisture and prevent water loss.

They also saw cacti-like plants with deep root systems that could tap into underground water sources. Some plants, like the acacia tree, had evolved long taproots that could reach deep below the surface to find water in a landscape where rainfall was almost nonexistent.

But Khalid's mood shifted when he began to discuss a more serious issue affecting the desert—desertification. He explained that desertification is the process by which

once-productive land becomes increasingly dry and barren, turning into desert-like conditions. While deserts like the Sahara have existed for millions of years, desertification caused by human activities, such as overgrazing, deforestation, and unsustainable farming practices, was spreading at an alarming rate. Khalid and his team of scientists were working to understand how this process was affecting local communities, wildlife, and the environment, and what could be done to reverse it.

Maya and Liam joined Khalid and his team in the field, assisting with research on how desertification was impacting the land. They helped plant drought-resistant trees in areas where vegetation had been destroyed, part of an effort to restore balance to the ecosystem. The team also worked with local communities to educate people about sustainable farming techniques, such as crop rotation and water conservation, to reduce the impact of desertification. It was clear that climate change was making the situation even worse, as rising temperatures and unpredictable rainfall patterns intensified the desertification process.

As they worked alongside the scientists and locals, Maya and Liam were struck by how interconnected everything was. Desertification didn't just affect the land; it impacted the animals, plants, and people who relied on the desert's resources.

Khalid explained that when the land becomes too dry to support crops or livestock, people are forced to move, often into cities or other areas, which can lead to overcrowding and further environmental stress. In addition, wildlife that once thrived in the desert, like antelopes and birds, was losing its habitat, making it more difficult for them to survive.

The children felt a deep sense of responsibility as they learned about the challenges the desert faced.

They understood that climate change was not just a distant problem but one that was already having serious consequences on ecosystems around the world. Maya and Liam were amazed by the resilience of the people who lived in the desert, and how they had adapted to these extreme conditions over centuries. But they also saw the urgency of the situation—if desertification wasn't addressed, the consequences could be devastating for both people and wildlife.

As the day ended, Khalid took them to a high sand dune to watch the sunset. The golden light bathed the desert in a surreal glow, casting long shadows across the dunes. Maya and Liam sat in silence, contemplating everything they had learned. The Sahara Desert, with all its beauty and harshness, was a reminder of the delicate balance of nature—and how easily it could be tipped by human actions.

They made a silent vow to continue raising awareness about climate change, desertification, and the importance of preserving the world's most vulnerable ecosystems.

That night, under a blanket of stars, Khalid shared stories of desert life and the legends of his ancestors, who had navigated the Sahara for centuries. The warmth of the fire and the vast, silent desert around them felt both comforting and humbling.

Maya and Liam knew they had witnessed something special. They had explored the desert's secrets, but they had also learned the importance of protecting it—because the Sahara, like so many other ecosystems, was not just a place to visit, but a place that needed care and attention if it was to survive.

Chapter 5: Saving the Forests of Borneo

Maya and Liam's next adventure took them to the tropical rainforests of Borneo, an island known for its lush jungles, incredible biodiversity, and unique wildlife. After arriving in Malaysia, they were greeted by their guide, Rina, a local conservationist who worked with endangered species in the region.

Rina explained that Borneo's rainforests are some of the oldest and most biologically rich forests in the world, but they are also among the most threatened.

As they journeyed deeper into the rainforest, Maya and Liam were in awe of the towering trees and the dense canopy above them. The air was thick with humidity, and the sounds of the jungle were alive with activity—the calls of exotic birds, the rustle of leaves as monkeys swung through the trees, and the occasional thud of a falling fruit.

One of the first animals they encountered was the famous orangutan. Rina led them to a sanctuary where orphaned and rescued orangutans were being rehabilitated before being returned to the wild.

Maya and Liam were immediately struck by how intelligent and gentle these creatures were. They watched as orangutans played and interacted with one another,

some swinging from ropes and others using tools to crack open coconuts. Rina explained that orangutans, who share about 97% of their DNA with humans, are highly intelligent and social creatures, but their populations are rapidly declining due to habitat destruction and illegal poaching.

Borneo is home to two species of orangutans: the Bornean orangutan and the Sumatran orangutan. The Bornean species, in particular, is critically endangered, with fewer than 15,000 individuals left in the wild. The main threat to these majestic creatures is the destruction of their natural habitats, primarily due to illegal logging and the expansion of palm oil plantations. Palm oil, a widely used ingredient in many products, has caused widespread deforestation, as large areas of rainforest are cleared to make way for oil palm crops.

Maya and Liam were shocked to learn that much of Borneo's rainforest, which had once been home to a wealth of wildlife, was now disappearing at an alarming rate. The palm oil industry, though economically significant, was having devastating effects on the environment. Not only were orangutans losing their homes, but other animals, like the pygmy elephants and proboscis monkeys, were also facing extinction due to the shrinking forests.

Maya and Liam knew they had to learn more about how they could help.
Their next stop was a rehabilitation center for orangutans, where they met a team of conservationists who were working tirelessly to rescue and care for the animals. They learned about the rigorous process of rehabilitation—how injured or orphaned orangutans are fed, given medical care, and taught the skills they need to survive in the wild.

Maya and Liam were given the opportunity to help by assisting in feeding the young orangutans and observing their interactions with the older, more experienced animals.

The children also learned about the importance of reforestation efforts. In areas where the rainforest had been destroyed, conservationists were working to replant native trees that would restore the habitat for orangutans and other species.

Maya and Liam joined the team in planting saplings, which would grow into large trees, offering a safe environment for wildlife in the years to come. Rina explained that these efforts were crucial not just for orangutans, but for the entire ecosystem, as the rainforests of Borneo play an important role in absorbing carbon dioxide and regulating the global climate.

In addition to the rehabilitation work, Maya and Liam helped raise awareness about sustainable palm oil. Rina showed them how local communities were being educated about the importance of supporting companies that used certified sustainable palm oil, which was grown on land that hadn't been cleared from rainforests. By buying products made with sustainable palm oil, consumers could help reduce the demand for unsustainable practices that contribute to deforestation.

The deeper Maya and Liam got into their work in Borneo, the more they understood the urgent need for conservation. They realized that protecting the rainforests of Borneo wasn't just about saving one species, like the orangutans—it was about preserving an entire ecosystem that supports countless forms of life. By working with conservationists, they saw firsthand how dedicated people were to making a difference, but they also understood that the task was enormous and required the cooperation of governments, businesses, and individuals worldwide. As the sun began to set over the rainforest, casting a golden glow through the trees, Maya and Liam reflected on all they had learned. They had seen the incredible beauty and richness of Borneo's rainforests, but they had also witnessed the devastating impact of human activity.

The threat of extinction loomed large over many species, and the destruction of these vital ecosystems would have far-reaching consequences. However, the efforts of passionate conservationists and local communities gave them hope.

That evening, as they sat with Rina and the rest of the team around a campfire, Maya and Liam discussed what they could do to help. Rina reminded them that every action counts,

whether it's supporting sustainable products, raising awareness about deforestation, or simply sharing the stories of the animals they had encountered. The children knew that they were just two people, but if everyone worked together, they could make a significant impact on saving the rainforests and the incredible species that call them home.

As they drifted off to sleep that night, the sounds of the rainforest echoed in the distance, a reminder of the vibrant life that still thrived in Borneo's rainforests—life that, with hard work and dedication, could be protected for generations to come.

Chapter 6: The Wonders of the Arctic Circle

Maya and Liam's final adventure took them to one of the most remote and stunning places on Earth—the Arctic Circle. After a long journey, they arrived at a research station located in the icy wilderness of the Arctic. They were welcomed by Dr. Elena, a scientist who specialized in Arctic ecosystems and wildlife. Dr. Elena explained that the Arctic is home to some of the most unique and resilient species on the planet,

but it is also one of the most vulnerable to the effects of climate change.
The landscape that stretched out before them was both breathtaking and stark. Towering icebergs floated in the frigid waters, their surfaces gleaming in the pale sunlight. Snow covered the ground in every direction, and the air was crisp and cold. Maya and Liam could hardly believe they were standing on the edge of the world,

surrounded by such beauty and harshness. The Arctic was unlike any place they had visited before.

Dr. Elena began their tour by introducing them to the wildlife that thrived in this frozen environment. Maya and Liam were thrilled to see polar bears, the undisputed kings of the Arctic. They watched in awe as a mother bear and her cubs carefully navigated the icy terrain, searching for food. Dr. Elena explained that polar bears are incredibly well adapted to life in the Arctic,

with their thick white fur, large paws, and layers of fat that help them survive the extreme cold.

"Polar bears rely on sea ice to hunt for seals, which make up most of their diet," Dr. Elena explained. "But with the warming climate, the ice is melting earlier in the spring and forming later in the fall, making it harder for the bears to find food."

Maya and Liam learned that polar bears were facing a dire situation. As the Arctic warmed, sea ice was disappearing at an alarming rate, making it increasingly difficult for the bears to find hunting grounds. The loss of sea ice was not just a problem for polar bears—it was impacting the entire food chain, including seals, fish, and even migratory birds that depended on the ice as a habitat.

As they continued their journey, Maya and Liam were introduced to another iconic Arctic species—the gray whale. They joined Dr. Elena and her team aboard a research vessel to track the movement of migrating whales. Every year, gray whales migrate thousands of miles from the warm waters of Mexico to the Arctic to feed on the nutrient-rich waters. However, climate change was affecting this migration. Rising ocean temperatures and changing sea currents were disrupting the whales' feeding grounds, forcing them to travel further and for longer periods.

While out on the water, Maya and Liam were able to witness

the awe-inspiring sight of a pod of whales breaching the surface, their massive bodies gliding gracefully through the water. The sight left them speechless, but it also served as a powerful reminder of the delicate balance that existed in the Arctic ecosystem. With climate change disrupting the food chain and altering migration patterns, these majestic creatures were facing an uncertain future. Maya and Liam also learned about the impact of melting ice on indigenous communities in the Arctic. The Inuit people, who had lived in the Arctic for thousands of years, depended on the ice for hunting, fishing, and transportation. As the ice melted, it became harder for the Inuit to travel across the land, and their traditional way of life was being threatened. Dr. Elena shared how scientists were working with local communities to find solutions that would help preserve the Arctic's cultural heritage while addressing the challenges posed by a changing climate.

The next part of their adventure involved helping a team of scientists track the movement of polar bears. They were taken to a field station where scientists were using GPS collars to monitor the bears' locations. Maya and Liam were amazed by the technology that allowed scientists to track the bears from miles away. With each bear's movements being recorded, researchers could gather crucial data about their behavior and the challenges they faced in the changing Arctic environment. One day, while out on an expedition with Dr. Elena and the team, they spotted a lone polar bear in the distance, moving across the ice. The team quickly set up equipment to monitor the bear's movements, and Maya and Liam were able to help by documenting the data.

It was an exciting and sobering moment—witnessing the bear's struggle to find solid ice and the way it carefully moved, searching for a place to hunt. They realized how critical it was for scientists to understand the impact of disappearing ice on polar bear populations and how essential it was to protect the Arctic habitat. Maya and Liam learned that the melting ice in the Arctic had global consequences. The region acts as a cooling system for the Earth, reflecting sunlight back into space and helping regulate global temperatures. As the ice melted, darker ocean waters were exposed, absorbing more heat and accelerating the process of warming. This “feedback loop” was causing temperatures in the Arctic to rise twice as fast as in other parts of the world, a phenomenon known as Arctic amplification. The children understood that what was happening in the Arctic didn’t just affect the region—it had ripple effects around the globe.

As their time in the Arctic came to a close, Maya and Liam were deeply moved by what they had learned. The Arctic was a place of stunning natural beauty, but it was also a region facing unprecedented challenges. The impacts of climate change were already being felt, and without urgent action, many of the species they had encountered, including polar bears and whales, could face extinction. But Maya and Liam also learned about the tireless efforts of scientists, local communities, and conservationists who were working together to protect the Arctic's fragile ecosystems.

On their final night in the Arctic, Maya and Liam stood outside, bundled up in warm clothes, and watched the northern lights dance across the sky in a mesmerizing display of colors. They reflected on their journey, knowing they had witnessed some of the world's most vulnerable ecosystems. But they also understood that protecting these ecosystems required more than just knowledge—it required action. Whether it was reducing carbon emissions, supporting conservation efforts, or spreading awareness about the importance of preserving the planet's most fragile places, they knew they had a responsibility to help.

As they boarded the plane back home, Maya and Liam felt empowered and determined to continue their environmental journey. The world's ecosystems were interconnected, and if everyone worked together, there was hope for a future where the wonders of the Arctic—and all of Earth's precious habitats—could be protected for generations to come.

www.ingramcontent.com/pod-product-compliance
Lightning Source LLC
LaVergne TN
LVHW041119150826
845673LV00007B/2127

* 9 7 9 8 2 2 7 5 4 1 1 3 0 *